Color My Coral
Activity Coloring Book
Illustrated and Designed by Heidi Joulios

Donated by
Martin Pearl
PUBLISHING
www.MartinPearl.com f
Visit our Teacher Resource page

Get ready to swim through a sea of amazing
coloring pages, mazes, puzzles and more!

It's a wave of fun!

The Young Explorer
This book belongs to

_____

Your name here

Text and Illustrations copyright © 2013 Heidi Joulios

A special "thank you" to Mark Deamer for front and back cover design.

First Edition
ISBN: 9781936528127

Published by
Martin Pearl Publishing
P.O. Box 1441, Dixon, CA 95620
www.martinpearl.com

Martin Pearl
PUBLISHING

PRINTED IN THE UNITED STATES OF AMERICA

10 9 8 7 6 5 4 3 2 1

Scuba Adventure Mask

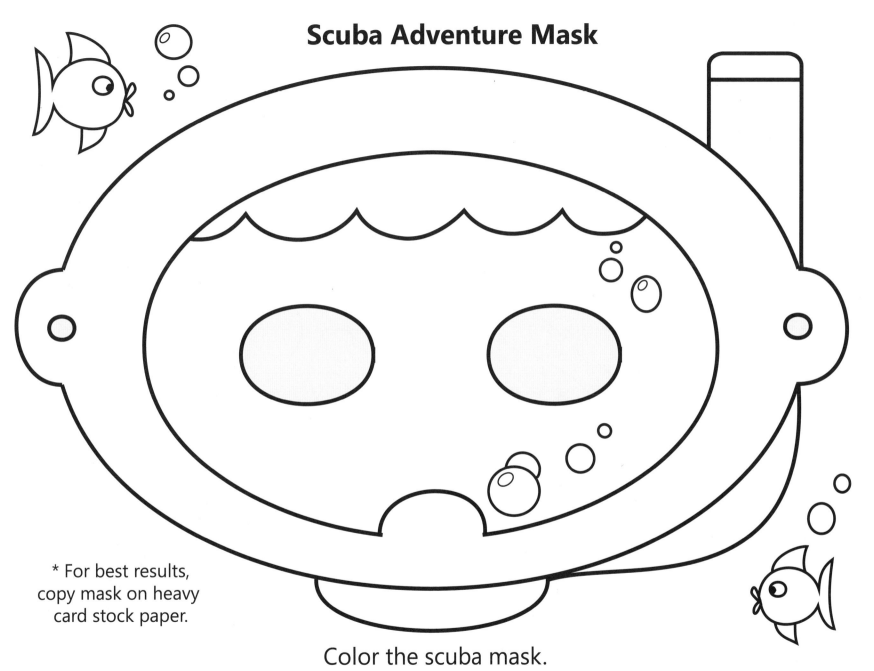

* For best results, copy mask on heavy card stock paper.

Color the scuba mask.
With adult assistance, use scissors to cut out the mask and shaded areas to make eye holes.
Punch out holes on both sides of the mask. Attach a string to fit around your head.

Loretta The Crab

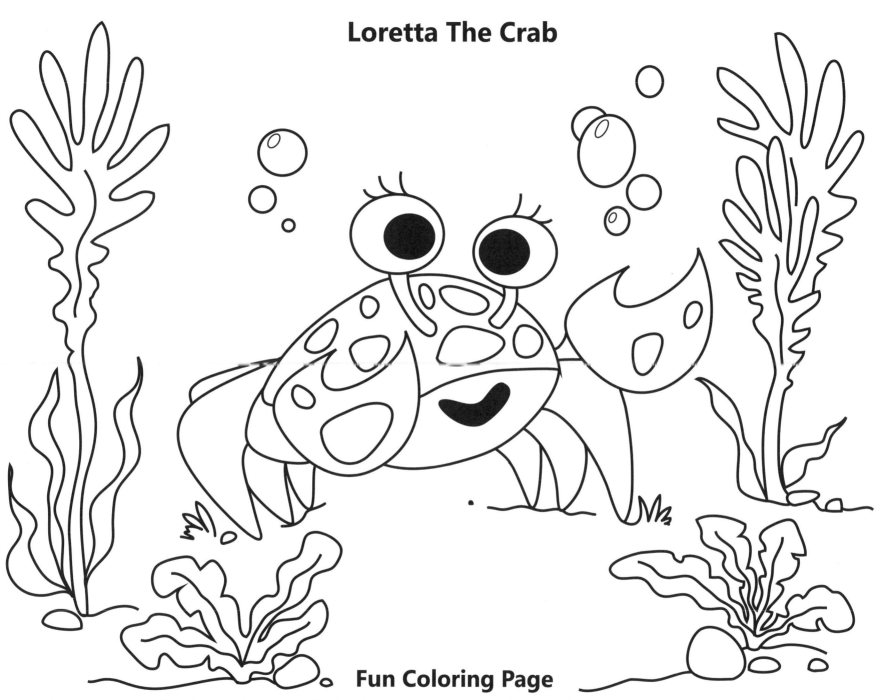

Fun Coloring Page

Crabs are small animals that mostly live in oceans, but can live on land. Some crabs have hard shells, and some have soft shells. All crabs have eight back legs, two front claws, and walk sideways.

Turbulent Seawater Maze

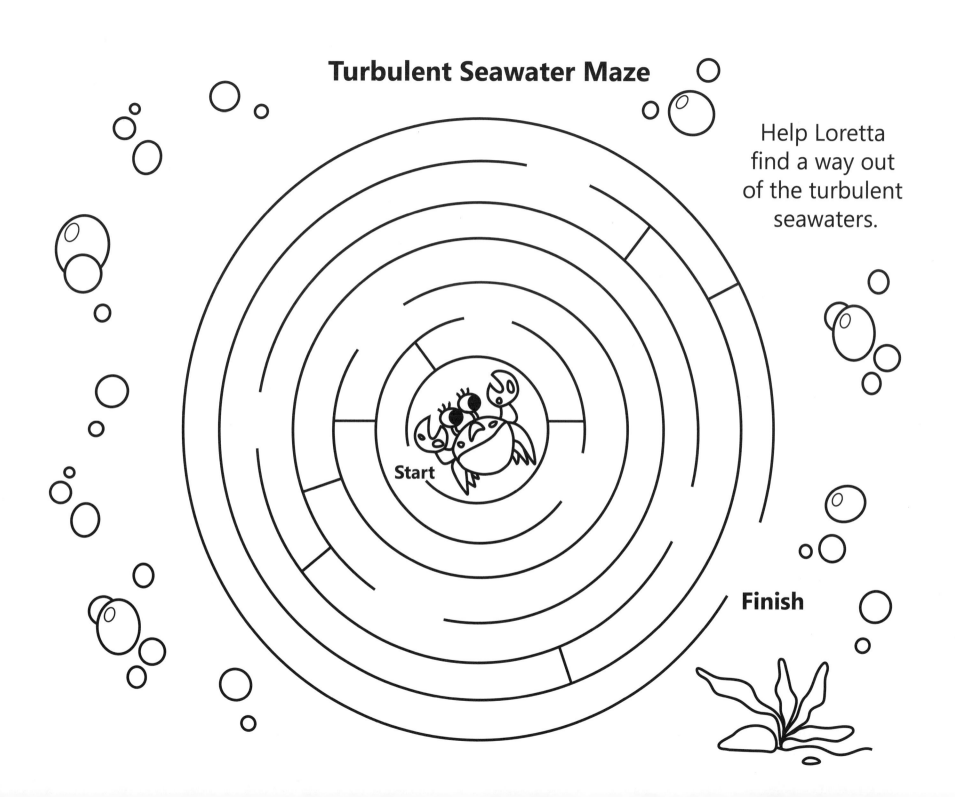

Help Loretta find a way out of the turbulent seawaters.

Start

Finish

Oliver The Sea Slug

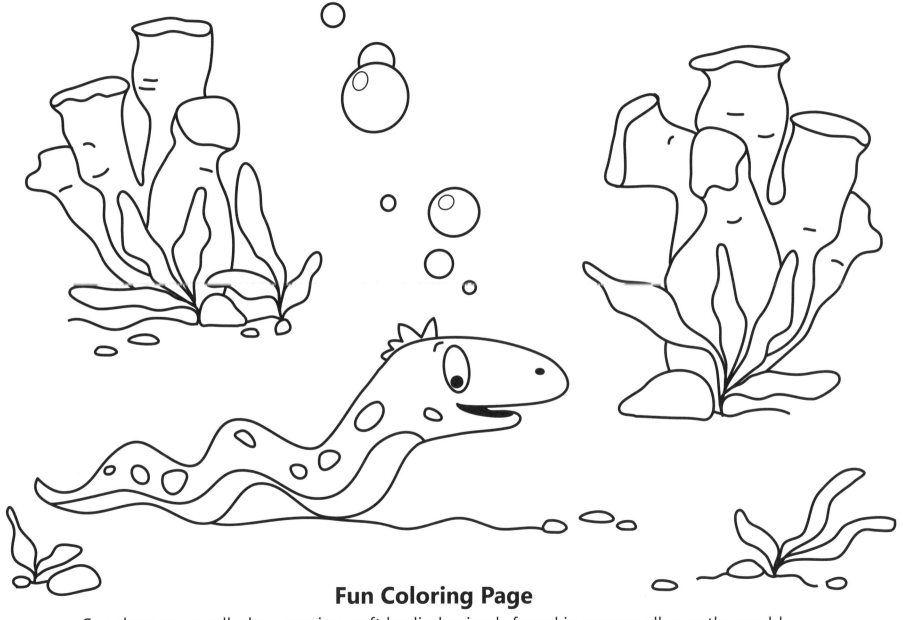

Fun Coloring Page

Sea slugs are small, slow-moving, soft bodied animals found in oceans all over the world.
Sea slugs look like snails, without a shell.

Color By Number

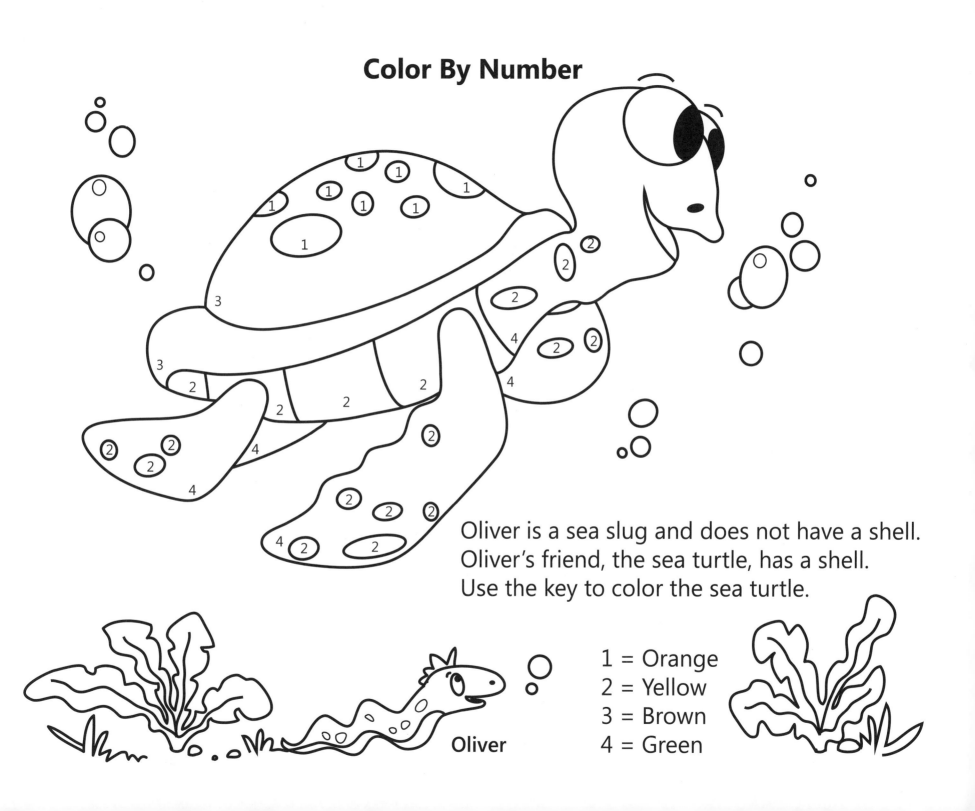

Oliver is a sea slug and does not have a shell.
Oliver's friend, the sea turtle, has a shell.
Use the key to color the sea turtle.

Oliver

1 = Orange
2 = Yellow
3 = Brown
4 = Green

A Snail's Race

Follow the lines to see which sea snail finishes the race.

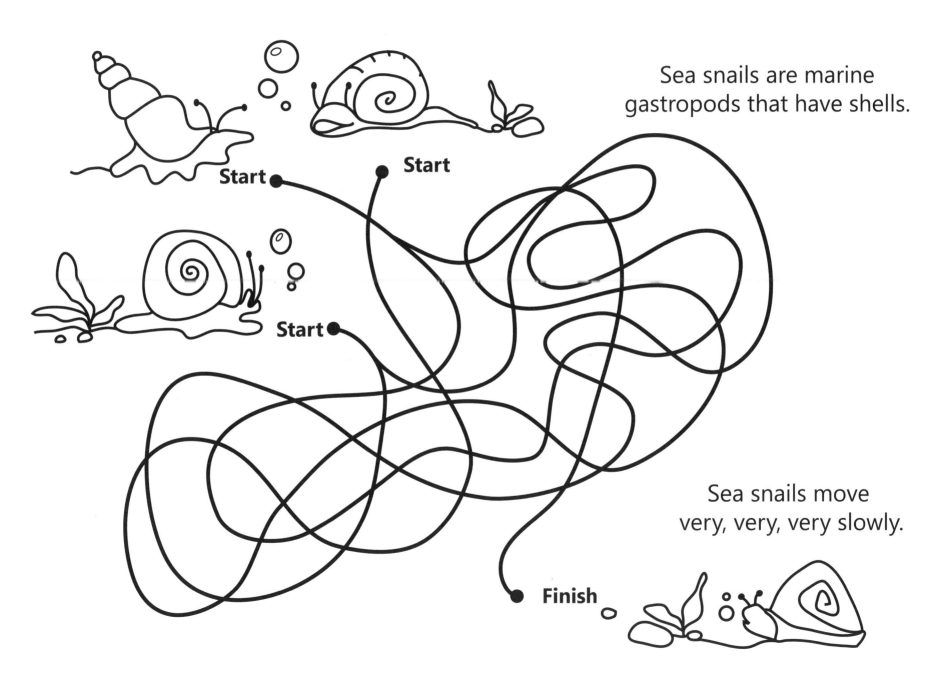

Sea snails are marine gastropods that have shells.

Start

Start

Start

Finish

Sea snails move very, very, very slowly.

Seabed Mystery Shape

Connect the dots.

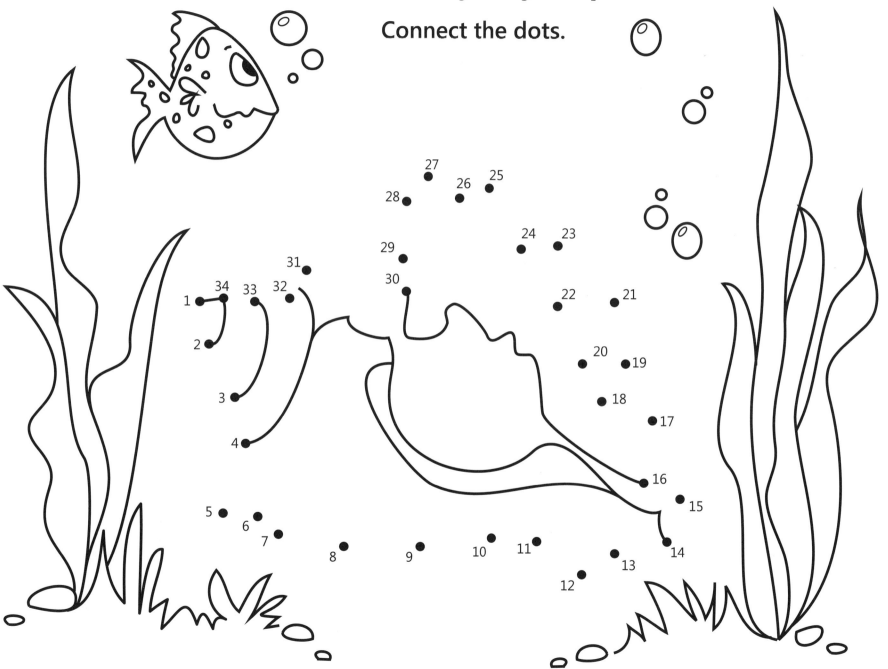

Dr. Eel The Moray Eel

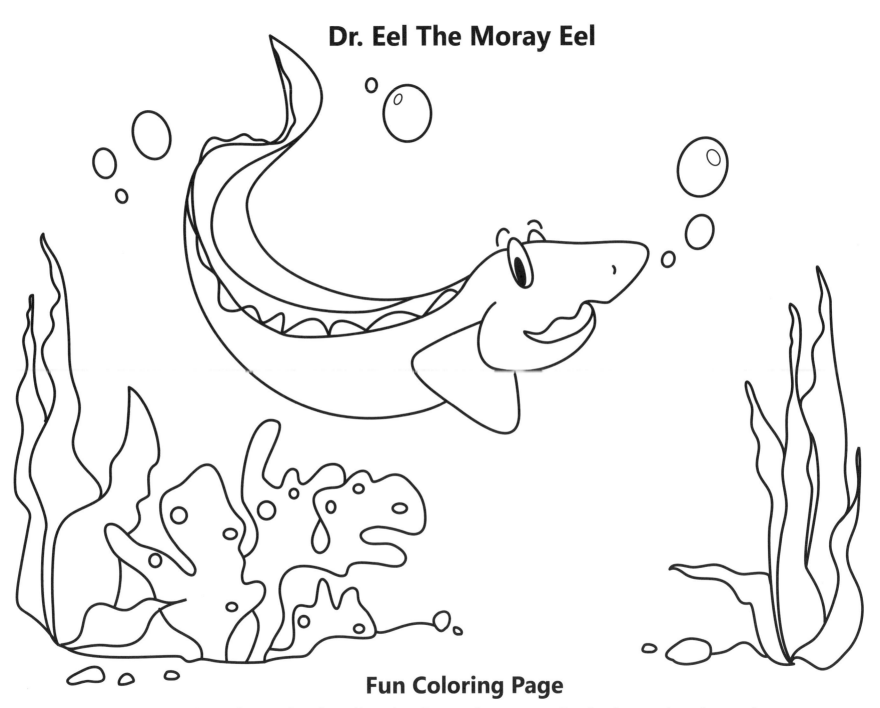

Fun Coloring Page

Moray Eels have long, slender, slimy bodies and can actually tie themselves into a knot.
Moray Eels may look like snakes, but they are fish.

Word Search

q l i a n s w o f
e l t r u t s x c
h b f o r a h j w
k m z y a r r u s
j e l l y f i s h
n w o r m i m h a
l e k a n s p a r
d m f i s h g p k

Coral Reef Sea Life

jellyfish
shrimp
shark
turtle
starfish
worm
fish
snail
ray
snake

Doctor Eel is teaching a school of fish about other creatures that visit the coral reef. To find the names of these sea creatures, look up, down, forward, and backward.

Betty The Lobster

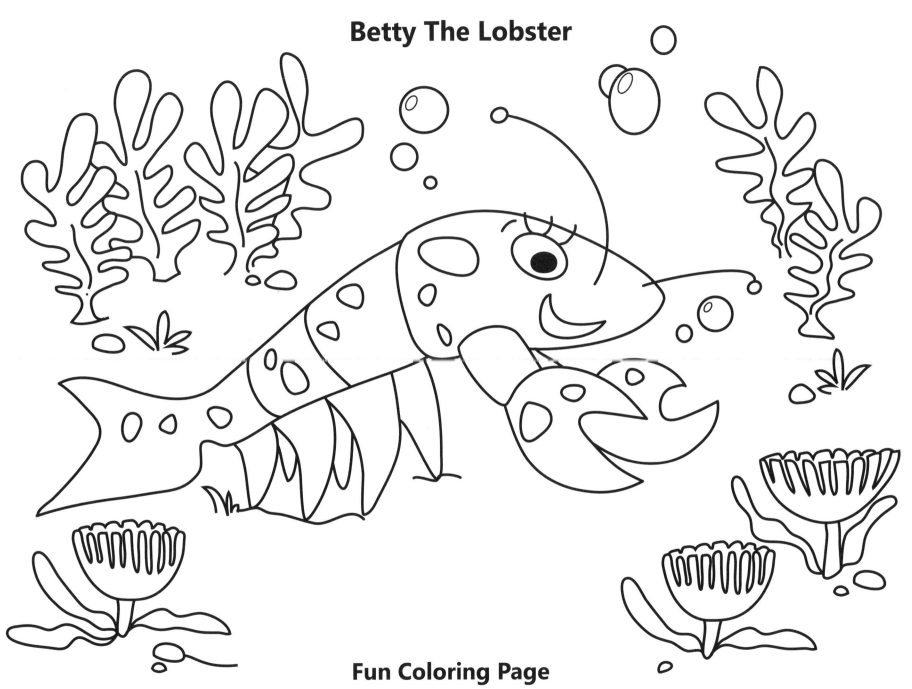

Fun Coloring Page

Lobsters are animals that live on the ocean floor.
Lobsters have ten legs, a hard shell and can live to be more than 50 years old.

Puzzling Coral Names

Coral can be found in many different shapes, sizes and colors.
A coral's name can describe what it looks like.
Help Betty solve the puzzle.

Draw a line to connect the coral to its name.

Organ Pipe Coral

Brain Coral

Branch Coral

Donut Coral

Bubble Coral

Daisy Coral

Betty

Puffed Up Patty The Pufferfish

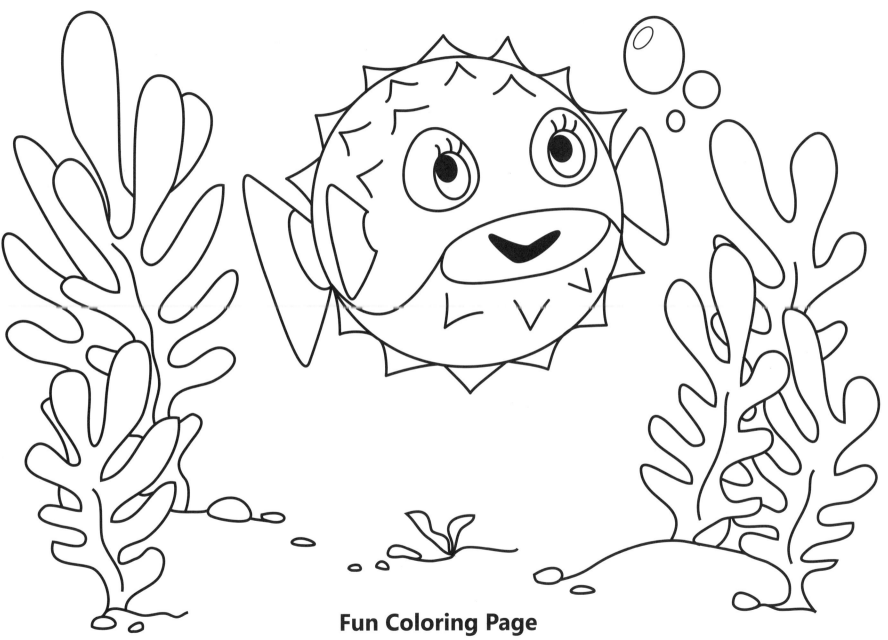

Fun Coloring Page

Pufferfish are also known as blowfish.
When a pufferfish is in danger, it will swallow water and then puff up, like a prickly porcupine.

Hide And Seek In The Reef

Help Puffed Up Patty find 10 things
that do not belong in the reef.
Color in the objects.

Sorting Game

People visiting the beach
sometimes leave items behind.
Draw a line to show
where these items should really go.

chip bag

pizza
slice

plastic
bottle

plastic bag

candy
wrapper

newspaper

glass
bottle

can

Helpful Hint
Food items and most food packaging belong in the trash.
Plastic, glass, aluminum, and paper items can be recycled.

Trash

Recycle

Seabed Shadows

Coral reefs are often called underwater gardens.
The seabed creatures below may look like plants, but they are really animals.
Can you match each sea creature with its shadow?

Sea Cucumber

Sea Anemone

Sea Sponge

Sea Urchin

Mushroom Coral

Lettuce Leaf Sea Slug

A Fishy Maze

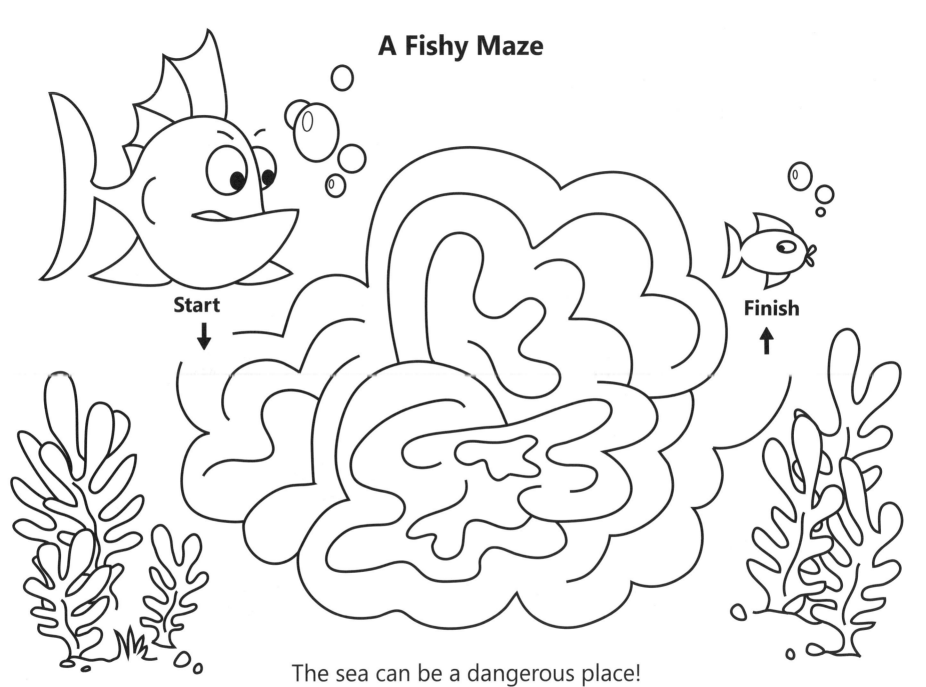

Start

Finish

The sea can be a dangerous place!
This little fish was a clever swimmer to escape the jaws of a large predator.
What path did the little fish take to escape?

Mystery Fish

Connect the dots.

This large fish has very sharp teeth and might be the most feared predator in the ocean.

Irwin The Sea Cow

Fun Coloring Page

Sea Cow is another name for Manatee. Manatees are large, friendly, slow-moving marine mammals.
Sea Cows spend most of their time grazing for plant food in the water, like cows do on land.

Word Search

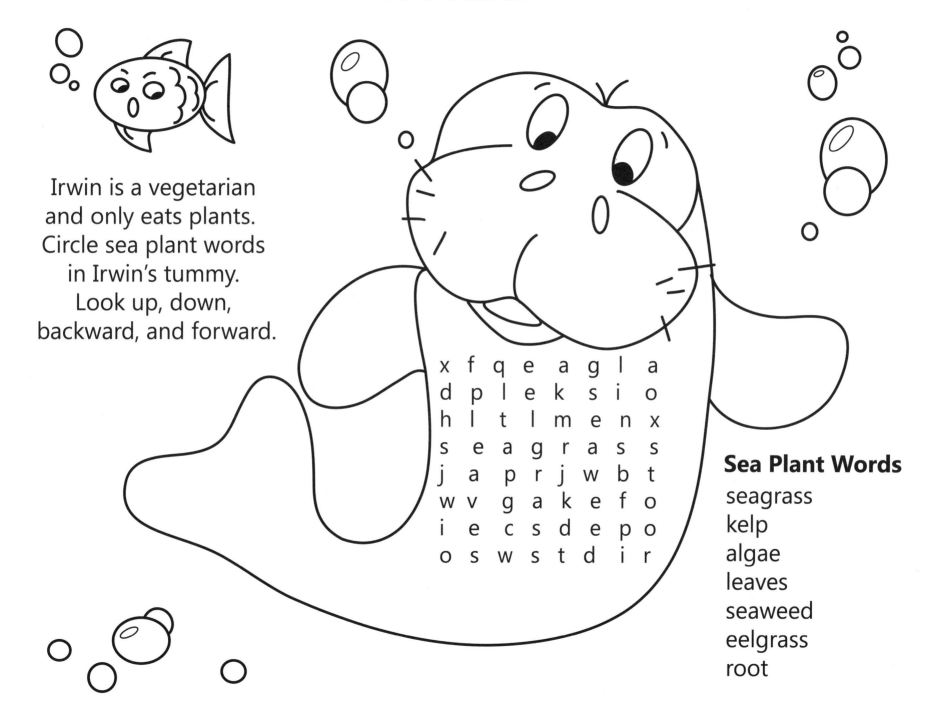

Irwin is a vegetarian and only eats plants. Circle sea plant words in Irwin's tummy. Look up, down, backward, and forward.

```
x f q e a g l   a
d p l e k s i   o
h l t l m e n   x
s e a g r a s   s
j a p r j w b   t
w v g a k e f   o
i e c s d e p   o
o s w s t d i   r
```

Sea Plant Words

seagrass
kelp
algae
leaves
seaweed
eelgrass
root

Arty The Octopus

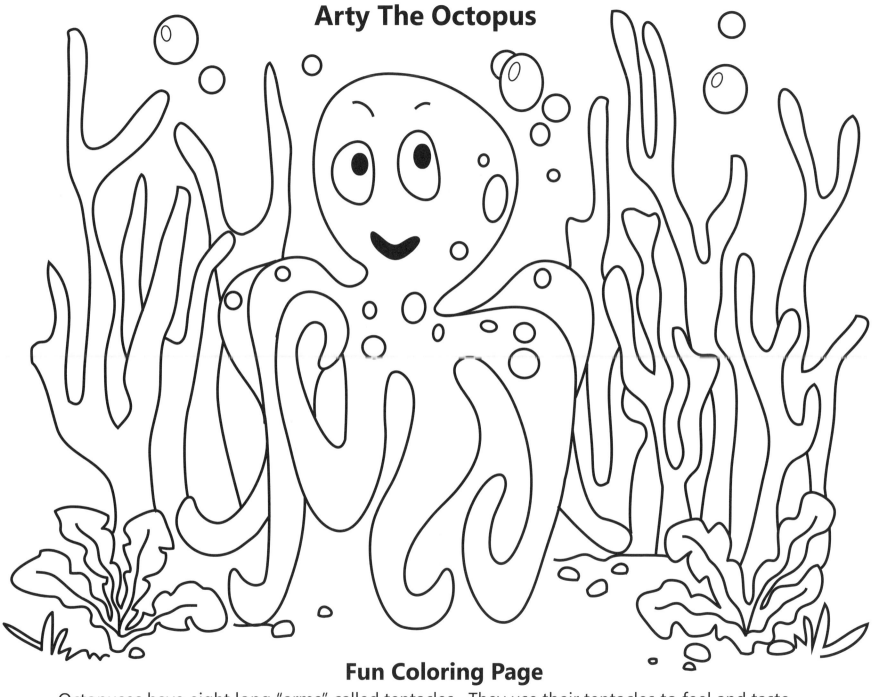

Fun Coloring Page

Octopuses have eight long "arms" called tentacles. They use their tentacles to feel and taste.
Octopuses live in oceans and can swim very fast by squirting water from their bulb-like bodies.

Create a masterpiece with Arty.
Draw and color an underwater scene
and fill it with your favorite
sea creatures.

A Coral Reef Masterpiece

Your name here

Answer Page

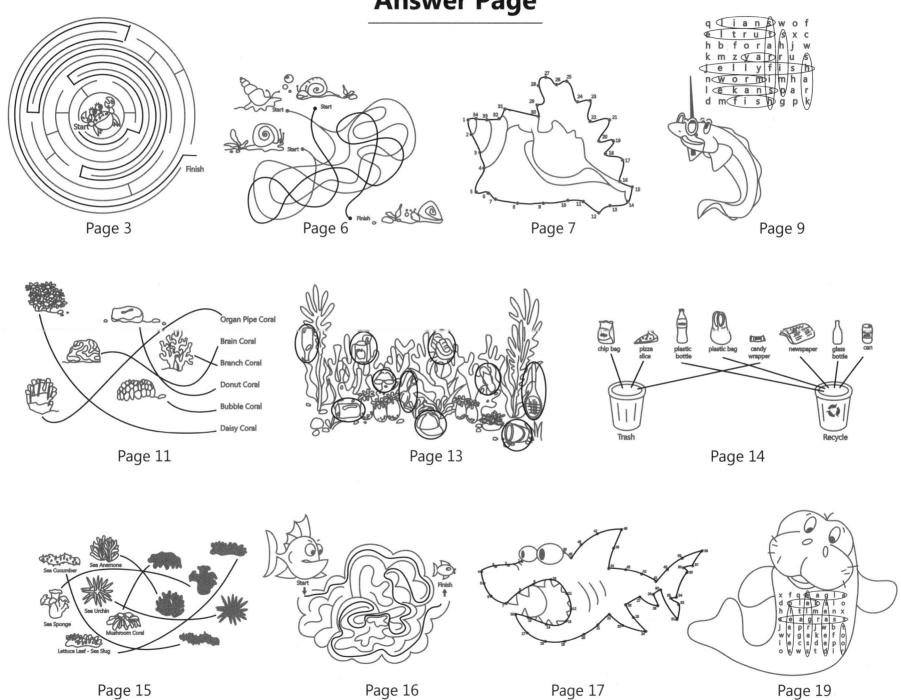

Page 3

Page 6

Page 7

Page 9

Page 11

Page 13

Page 14

Page 15

Page 16

Page 17

Page 19